The Top Jobs

By Daisy Hawkins

ned in 2026 by
vood House Press
Clinton Street
, NY 14224

l in the United States of America

Library of Congress Cataloging-in-Publication Data:
Names: Hawkins, Daisy, author.
Title: Top Jobs ; They March at Night / written by Daisy Hawkins.
Description: Buffalo, NY : Norwood House Press, 2026. | Series: Phonics all-stars: phase 3 |
Identifiers: ISBN 9781978578081 (pbk.) | ISBN 9781978578098 (library bound) | ISBN 9781978578104 (ebook)
Subjects: LCSH: Reading–Phonetic method–Juvenile literature. | English language–Phonetics–Juvenile literature. | Soccer–Juvenile literature. | Occupations–Juvenile literature. | Soldiers–Juvenile literature.
Classification: LCC LB1573.3 H395 2026 | DDC 372.465–dc23

CPSIA compliance information: Batch #CW26NHP: For further information contact Norwood House Press at 1-800-237-9932.

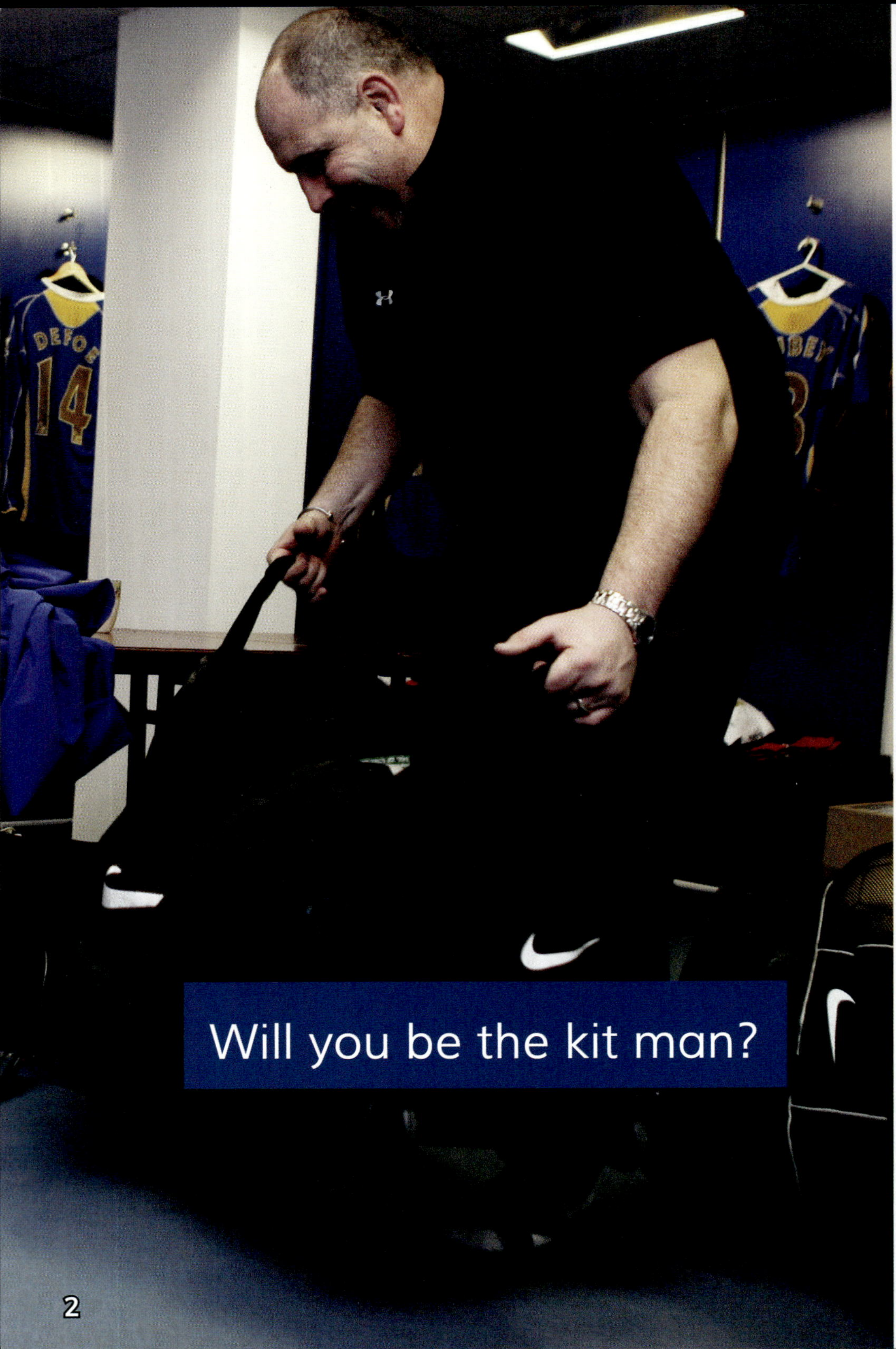

Will you be the kit man?

He gets the kit on the pegs.

Will you check the tops, the pads, the socks, and the boots?

Will you get rid of the locker room mess too?

Will you be the cook?

To keep fit, players need the right food.

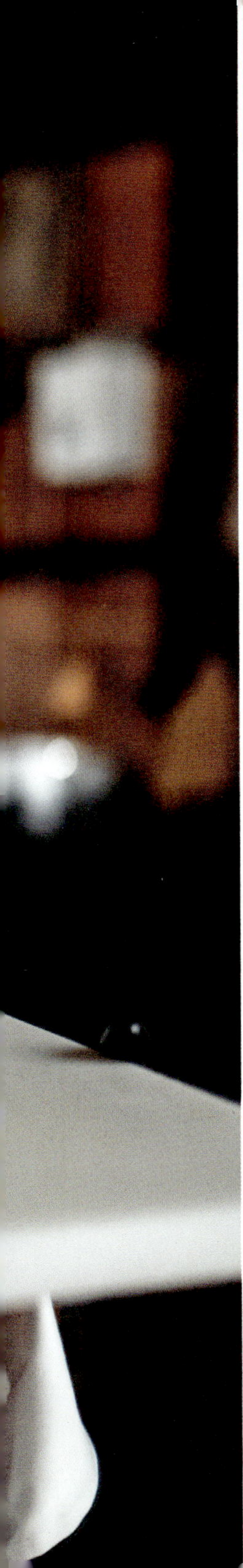

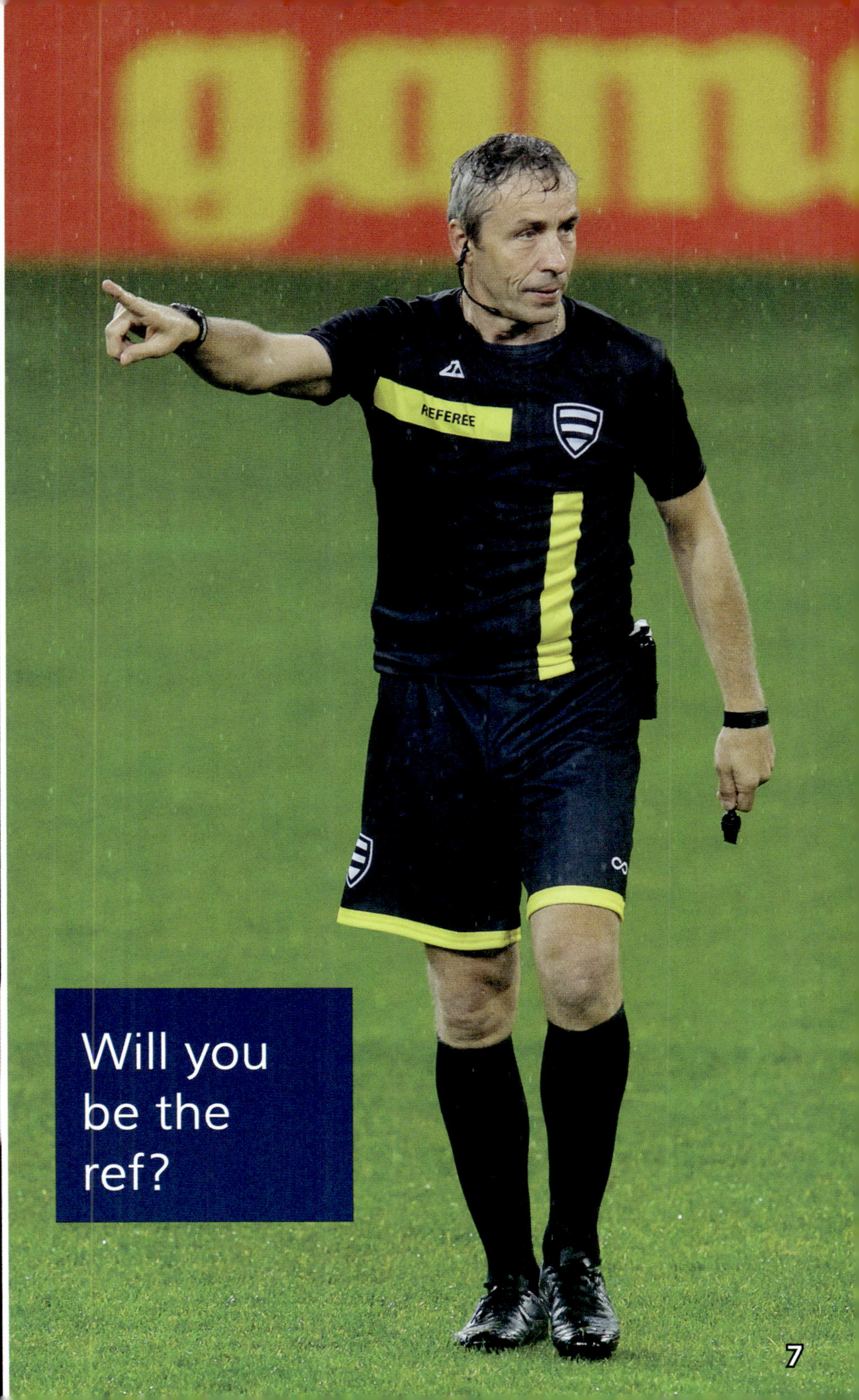

Will you be the ref?

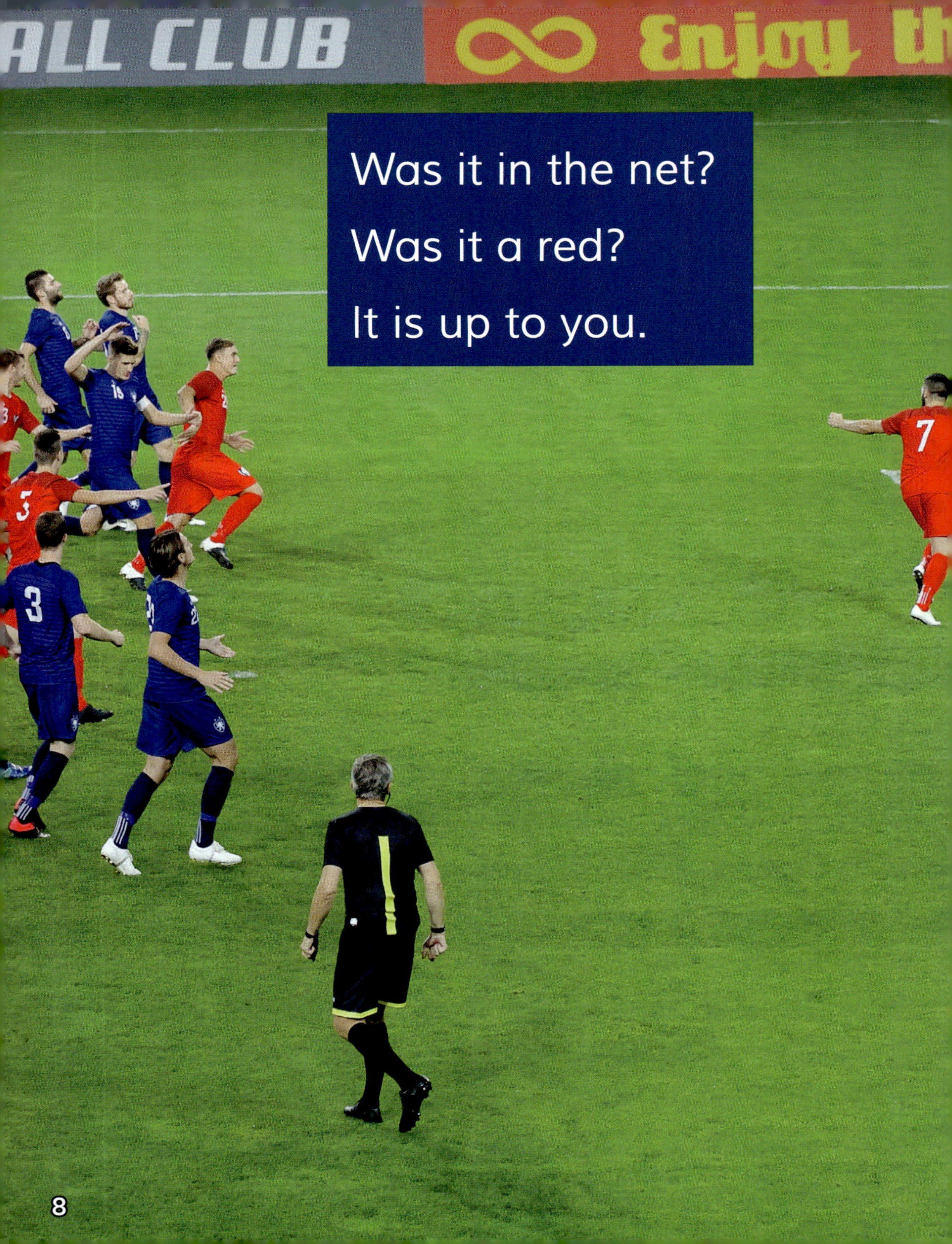

Was it in the net?

Was it a red?

It is up to you.

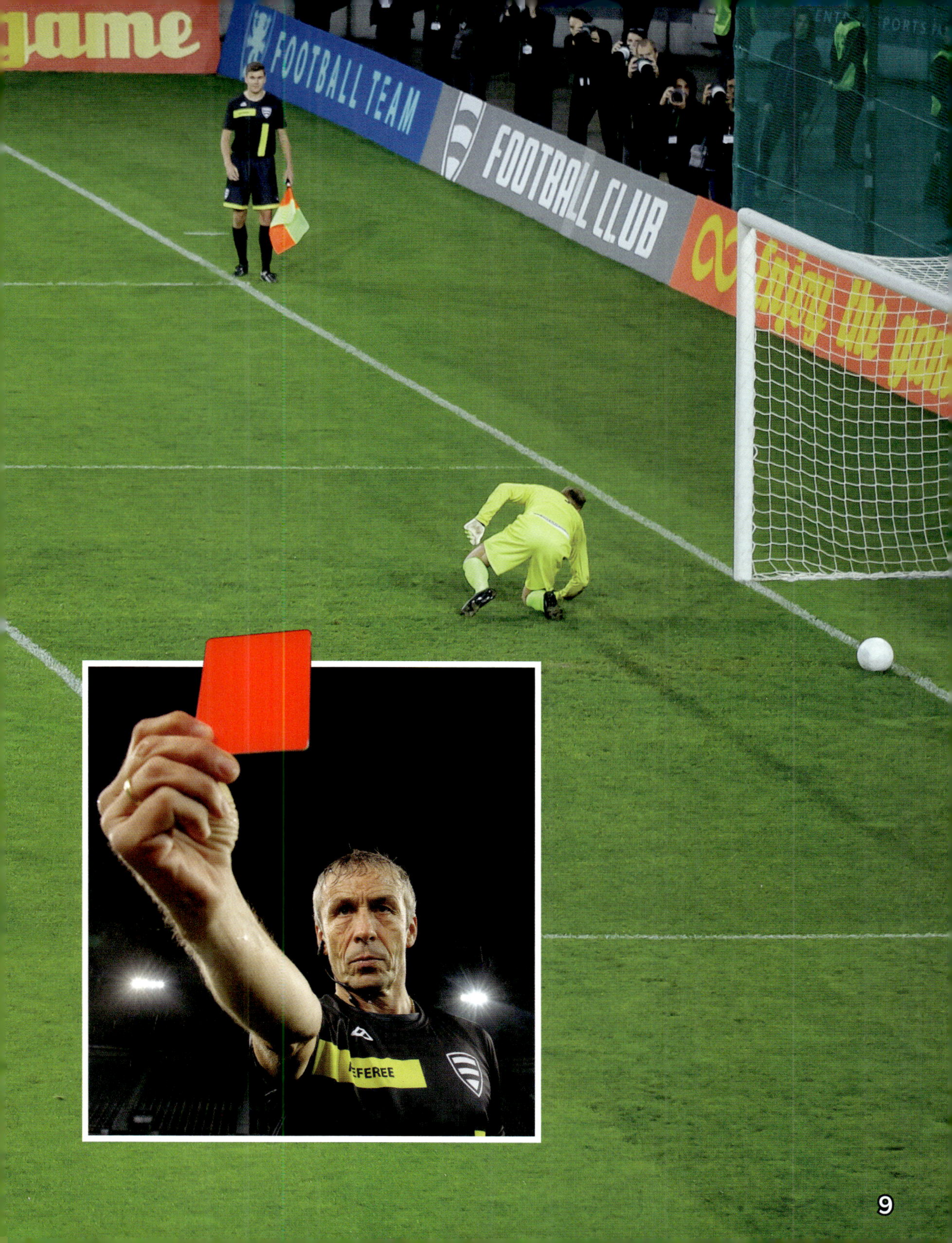
game
FOOTBALL TEAM
FOOTBALL CLUB

Will you be a fan?
Look, this fan took a pal.

It is fun to get food and sing songs, but if the ref is bad, the fans will boo.

Will you boo as well?

The kit men, cooks, refs, and fans did such a top job.

Did you?

They March at Night

Written by
Daisy Hawkins

Illustrated by
Ashleigh Green

It is a long road to the
hill fort in the north.

They march on foot
and they can not turn back.

This is the king's wish.

The moon is high and the
chill night is thick with fog.

In the dim light of the moon, they see a shed.

Is it a farm hut?

Or is it **them**, not in the hill fort but in this shed, to shock the king's men?

They march on, up to the shed, and check it.

They can not see **them**.

It seems, then, that this fight will be at the hill fort.

They wait a bit, then
turn and march on.

In the dark of the night
it is hard to see.

They all feel the rain as it
turns to hail.

They march on. It is the king's wish.

They can not go back.